t & u & lash your nipples to a post history is gorgeous

Jared Schickling

t &u& lash your nipples to a post
history is gorgeous

Jared Schickling

BlazeVOX [books]
Buffalo, NY

t&u& lash your nipples to a post
history is gorgeous by Jared Schickling
Copyright © 2011

Published by BlazeVOX [books]

Printed in the United States of America

Book design by Geoffrey Gatza

First Edition
ISBN: 978-1-60964-069-9
Library of Congress Control Number: 2011908994

BlazeVOX [books]
76 Inwood Place
Buffalo, NY 14209

Editor@blazevox.org

publisher of weird little books

BlazeVOX [books]

blazevox.org

2   4   6   8   0   9   7   5   3   1

BlazeVOX

ACKNOWLEDGMENT

Thank you, many times, C. J. Martin and Ash Smith at *Little Red Leaves*, Michael Mann at *unarmed*, and Jonathan Skinner and *Interim*, for publishing some of these, the Big Other blog and Mark Young at *Otoliths* for using the back-cover image and Michael Leong for supplying me with the bulk of that material. Thank you Geoffrey Gatza. Thank you, Mollie. Thank you, all the writers mentioned or otherwise in the text.

CONTENTS

t&u& lash your nipples to a post

history is gorgeous

and whoever believes that one tracks down some *thing*? one tracks down tracks

EPIPHYTIC

If you got rid of the pressure to build to consume upon consuming
more
ways of

building then labor would not be obsolete this mosquito would be
natural
and people

would hate building beyond certain Maine as refuse uses

the trees and has been short time my old employer said everyone
w/

unused land or land in re-growth which seems to be everyone
hires

a forester a law to consult my friend calls

that one ironwood what the hell ironwood fresh
scrap's on the floor   the power's easy

where the dogs' are   poor connection

weightless line what   in strong rain

kind man does not

unleash dogs free

your boss turn domestic back

to something wld who can handle it (will handle them

damned mosquito)look
up

a woodpecker(muss

be)biggest

north america(who the
weightless)munching

beech beach look soft and hospitable and different too "carpenter"
mosses

(though its bark can go smooth crawlers re
blanket
beech tree falls the way it birch leans clearing to cedar instead
          versal (

of oak maple and willows of   malay proverbs ync us a

blueberry rather than appleniagara)

which were all hear too gron

(not even winter)taller and

top-heavy

the cherry tomatoes surprisingly orange and good)sometimes

heave

impressive radii   )of the moments
          "location location location

to wet perpetual youth is this strange bright summer's lovely dark
the freak

in s'old. Like Maine's public mountain you don't sea whose
stump abound
s'ndr

soft fern THE

LIBERTY INSTINCTUALrt   prtcptn

for

lovers'

sleeping, change   plstc

of

nation

panic re

store nothng

too

gone, morning

mourning for

arts

nos HERMIT

S' MASCOT FOR THE NEW EXPEDIENT BEHAVE
LSHD OUT BEHIND POETICST ALL
a guide to gentlme an so   pplst

halve you "frmrs
shll "cstdl

labore   wrtng n
won t   th wll str

m akes elf piss
cptl   p t t

edu
mns
pro

deuced elf its
u "frmngtn p

is sin to
knight mare w

o n t
        he ory

capit—
                        alors

log's happening

                              "fr

fair down

street thinks

must be

there class fall

began

things hay   brn   ng

everywhere

jobs   msss

over you

just have to wait for it u

are out here

marc use

a parent

backw

everywhere

a clearing that you no

where how ever   mstr

linwood's lone rnt

stars out seams

glad *call names*

very dry *and balance*

summer"

DISAPPOINTMENT *liar using contractions and gestures because it is comfortable in trth*

small things

moist pontless

how theys peak hear pg

turner

pens

be cause pen

is pen

shit look at your

climb out of

i am supposed to mean

you can't watch war TICKETS TO THE PINES

there is a femur not in the newspaper   to suck on it gray

there are fifty whales to kiss them   beach in new zealond

in central maine there is no femur   are whales close by

neither is there much   are hidden by the trees

neither though   a fair

MY HAIBUN

work week

they publish poetry

is a notebook

THE PRINCIPLE

It is physically impossible to measure the position and momentum

of a particle all at once. I would go with her

down to the canal

the east edge of town

the old, kept part

like a vale

this corridor

but I don't think about that anymore. I'm on

to better things. Even

bigger. In the drawer

is a ring

and no one even knows

which put it there. This

I feel calls for a style

correlating objectively

to the price of that thing

raised by recent studies

an investigation into

the rapes of 200 Raised by something cld

SUPERFISCAL uncertain teas   "beer beer beer

and this was the pointethe supply of such rings

be a property of actual   tightly controlled

features of the universe.   there are mountains of their parts.

seed Dub

ethno-   "self-poetics, our kind
(c. 1976 rpt. 2010)

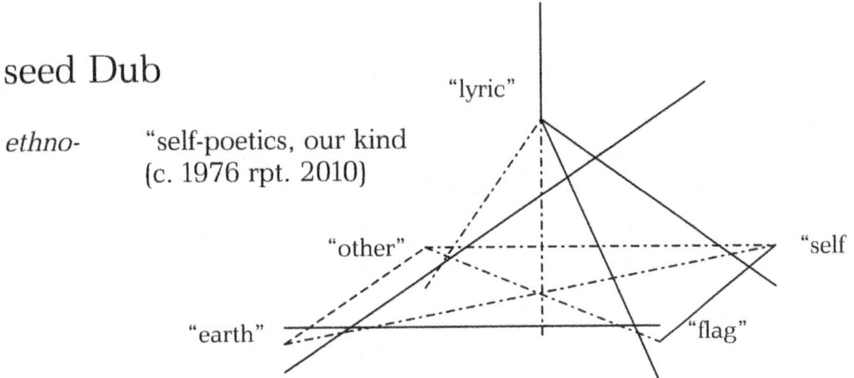

"by any other name

There was here and there a little knot and a few stragglers a few
yards higher up but they were so few as not to disturb the
simplicity and unity and life of that one busy highway."

" [skip that one.] "

"Pages ages page ages page ages."

AFTER BLEEPING SOMETHING

"but don'   t expect the poem to feed you"

—Michael Leong

1.

After writing something
close the fridge, go to sleep in your room.

2.

Close the door.

3.

After writing something, think
good. These were the parts I ordered.

4.

5.

You know No me.

6.

It took debt up the ass and the attendant wonder to realize
something simple.

7.

We know what we.

8.

9.

something went After writing something

10.

(whisper in the friend's ear

11.

tithe me,
not them.

MULE CALL & SQUEEGEE RESPONSE & WATER WARS PAVING THE WAY'S THE ARSE VIVID

for Jerrod Bohn post- ████████████

Bone Chitlin be no monster.
He just ate really strange poor
posture. Bone Chitlin contributes by 6 "pm"
mornin Bone Chitlin does not exist
then, Bone Chitlin knew us almost
all the time. Bone Chitlin would never say
"most of your time." Nor beliefs in lyin because
believin's good as he was
Bone Chitlin's around all the time.
His object dragged from me to find orbit
drive, insist it's meat.

Nothing was boredom, the boredom of life!
Dull freedoms of the ███ !
Black pools nothing bored!
Nothing drifting from the freezing blue sky!
Sober in the drought of the climbing moon!
██████ Nothing
was boredom, the boredom of life!

He'd insist that that's meat?
He promised mornin make a poem for his mother
's feat Bone Chitlin only did this because
were things we can't fit together
because, Bone Chitlin din pat himself on the back.
Bone Chitlin could never pat his own back Bone
Chitlin was not that
's how She was she   failed?
             loved so much
Hymn Bone straight from his mother
's touch no wonder Bone
Chitlin's in love?

Paltry, so paltry would be ███████ life—
a squalid king w/ credits!
Silver! he would stand under the roof of bright days
noisy he would give birth as the youngest king
closing his credited ears!
The boredom of life!

Bone Chitlin finds my crown for his mother.
Bone Chitlin don' pat hisself in the back.
Bone Chitlin rarely knew
what Hymn Chitlin's doin.
Who's in love with our wife but to whom car   nations
romance was never mprtnt
Bone Chitlin's sure in love with no thing at night's our ▆ that
she came as course gravel
bone debris as fertile ocean
buried under a road where Bone Chitlin found him pave
ment He traveled through muscle and bought his (diamonds
to know the inner workings of my heart.

stones in a croc's gut)   No, from morning's sun the first
message no more darkens ▆▆
water leaches at my starting gut.
No, much more blood from ▆▆
you earth, forgot people, vomit water
water from the sour morning's sun.
Nothing was boredom, the boredom of life.

Barely dead, not yet you freeze in the dawn ice.
Nothing from the sky is blue, not the sky or lands
emptying water, there's blood
blood buried in innocence here.

3 COLORS PLUS A VASE WAITING ANIMALS

He will water this what is most difficult to water it is in the other
room under th

floorboards look up or around trcky

chck is coming next week mollie won't cook me food yess

she will we love that therefore he buys flowers on my lunch brake
that

confession to their urinal's a glass case chck was

coming next week really just a memory

our love is in the other room

                      discussion (

emersons again which

proven's her point we

do have a dick but are not one even chck look

chck would prefer thoreau my

lv is not in this room flowers

still at work which was the intention by noon today car

nations his sun at its zenth tomorrow

forgetful as nothing

s in it

for you

NEW WAR SHOT 2 POEMS I SEE HER ON THE WAY TO
WORK, W/ NO KIDS,

OR OLD STORY OR EROS BLAMES IN THE TREES

worlds are ending   ONCE A DAY

no doubt is   HER DOOR CLOSES

about this uncertainty what i mean   ON A CITY

that there ending   ABOVE SOMETHING
LIGHTED

anticlimax can't even   RATS

sustain itself it needs ur this

thinking

about it

does not

stop talking   WHAT SNEAKING. SHE MAKE

put my   A GLUE TRAP SWEET ALMOST
                 BIG THE FEELING LESSER SHADOWS
gloves on

today feared

many things which

they expected no internal   LEAVING HER JOY.
                                     IF SHE IS NOT OR NOT
would write power   IN JOY REPELLING

lies where   ONE OLD FIX

gathering lives

don't go there   that is, on the forest floor
                    WOULD NOT HAVE BEEN LEFT NO
              GIVEN SHE
whole   DON'T LEAVE NOR GIVE THIS (SHE)
WAS

thing   HER NIGHTMARE. BUT

26

thing   IT CERTAINLY DOES

enclosed

open little   NOT KNOW A RAT NO

swift learned

how to   SWEET GLUE

wing it   ONCE A DAY

's failure common   (IT) COMES

explosion big y'll   TO HER DOOR

put all this together   OR WAITS

because it drives these from

selection

LETTER TO GRACE PALEY

have you seen anything happen while you were alive

have you gone through countless selves affirmation

have you heard how the sickles through the brown sweet hays

was silent in a poem

what have I done

not having sex in six months

have you made this up

there is a mirror in the bathroom

and you both look into it

on a daily basis the

look was simple

language little

family poo

sheep's family

RECORDED FUTURE *to be read allowed*

with a furrowed brow

RECORDED FUTURE

In-Q-Tel discovered in   queue tell the ink you
Recorded Future   toll the inc's
like Keyhole the beginning   on the wall
of Google Earth Christ   "Facebook
is beautiful
but he casts an extraordinary shadow"

                                        if you cannot read
this
bullshit. Christ is a baby sacking the Temple   who can help you
thank g-d well

are you that
tired
in the morning
know how we(e)k
you are

that
the b(e)acon
like
the radio

no care that   true, infinite, imagine, loving
responsibly, caringly, hole heartedly could
love that so
this

alphonso lingis says song or melody silences noise
he had an aviary
background noise

account for it c
age nails love   here here little birdie
bites

and taunts you   Russo
and eats you   Schapira
and denies it   Schelling
will make you   Schickling

hate them   Skinner
for denying it   Snyder
taunts you not because   Spahr
you were anything   Stuart1.
important   Taylor

took a shot of   little tombstones
all your houses
see it in my office "why
is poetry so boring" (Baraka)
was the subject of
books

that won 't work itself indeed
new to course to (so i'm told
can't muster no attention
reading of "Recorded Future" a company tracking reel internets
action in
orders to
"pre-dic the future (pre
dict-our future   "narcissistic
tendencies in many
investiture "Google   people fuel a need to have
domestic Intelligence   a large group of friends
lovely et al r us men-t   and many of these accept
t ions it since   they don't even know
wearing it won-t   this provided an excellent
forget Nabokov remark about "dim   vantage point for us
brained brutality which   to observe the daily
thwarts its own purpose techn-   life of beneficiaries
phili a c re ligion conviction "virtuality   of wild ass
-s the future   and petitioners of
fraudulent
-s @
last dream before
bed never wpd
this down   activities"
computer

(past.)(?)

"Rethink Oil" (some of us a   Day of ACTION POETS
"Rethink ~~Oil~~" or   jesus murphy)
~~oil~~

"a day of action"
NYC.   Albanys p
im   p   are a cites
                home town excuse
me i'm rusty
(vacation)   "That meaty flavor you tasted was most
likely iron

                    many stones in New England contain
"living in urban   copious amounts of iron it bleeds
centers challenges out of the rocks"
blah blah blah   or not—heavy metal "Manhattan
                    remember?   propped by forces
unseen"

(or not. 1 Love
canal.)

[Benjamin writing to the widemouth angel looking back caught
                          a gust of rising wind of pro
            grass Paradise with greater frequencees piling
                          representations perhaps
                    he sees there a nonexistence
                          of critical mass.]

future is nuclear
go head make
the poem
out of tru~~th~~
~~ad~~mires Thom Donovan
stays away. Or kari edwards as
they say but only after she they
will hate u and that
is because a grenade
had been put into their orifice *i bloc*
upon hearing *criticism thus*   *the conspiracy against*
poems
that the $ *screwed*
to be made has played
nice we love you
was what they say

LANGUAGE SCHOOL

one teacher early ·
on said up
there docs and
manifestos "i hate
nature" what a
wonderful man also
"it makes me
sic" was proven
(or even accepted
that old hystor   onomi)
in words as
things refer to
selves and all
that it has
wonderful hi up
view pond office
still must feel
cloisters for its
school was never
accepted much that
hadn't changed a
clean coffeemaker a
cab driver he
was and pushed
its people in
1 brilliant essay
after another so
what a man
history is gorgeous

· if you read this again, you will really see it is love's fruit, an eco-temporal flag in the ground

would inquire into the nature   "exhausted boy soldier reads book
numb
of "acceptance" like what does   rag head taken off by stiff
light·
that mean can   fig one triumph of the we're"
make a living
by avoiding its

first known mention
of jerusalems comes
from an execration text and doesn't even try face
up, pharaoh, launch
a shell don't
bear no bomb

· slip away

                              [relate news paper to front
                                           matter

· "whole.prism.to.circumscribe.another.composed.
·.of.prisms.so.that.the.circumscribed.figure.exceeds."

chthonic ON DOROTHEA LASKY'S *POETRY IS NOT A PROJECT*

"I think poems are living things that grow from the earth into the brain, rather than things that are planted within the earth by the brain."

interrupt (
rumble o
poetry
shit

)

of that
certain.
"

CAN i USE RELIGIOUS IMAGERY
is tool for take the joy
out
"only emotion objectified endures"
[parodied]

First thought when riding this who
prints this therefore is worth it think
Blake whose marriage wood
get it right
no need to correspond anything

Walk down the street and there Mc
artsy wood
side of the road Core
mac wed her irish on purpose
on the end of it

Under the arches
a public execution

Not of our time
deaths

the color is read
and yellow
patina, a burgher

your wife is slightly overweight
and your ankles are huge
they are sturdy you'd kill for her
you would of course turn away   boil on the butt
eat tulips in disguise
and lash your nipples to a post, a maypole but
morning's fair sight

should we leave at that
self-replicating

"one should not sleep anymore" pascal
wing tek lum
but not shepherd

i would write
what is not
easy to write   witch hazel & cream
we spread it
around and spend
nights never hating
the murder

each
fair
sight

SELF REPLICATING even the most extreme consciousness of
doom threatens to degenerate into idle chatter.

Because I want this new century to be full of people who write
poems, not full of poets who conduct projects and do nothing
more.

all these cloying
apologies   why be honest
the rare strategy
love's leader

iii ·

witch hazel and cream

DOMESTIC PROCEDURE the kind of boy you used to
close your eyes
birth canal

reach into [shorts] skirts and make from
scratch hung in the air exactly the way bricks don't

TECHNICIAN make
& leave the roots on, dangling

life less believable
calculate use
not to alarm   "a pain they have never dreamed of
there was a wall

"had heard or had heard said or had heard said written

shucking   fell   shudder   shift   crossing
            huffing
boil on the butt   rattle and clank   knobclick
            coallacking

@ EACH REMOVE shunting
moan

sacred bawling due briefs time

frame ATRAZINE lrnng
                                                          beard dreads or
                                                          clean baby's
shave space   bottom corn
                                                          row fields

multitude's head
bloody boy's filled the bloody bath with bloody snakes again

"if we do not find anything very pleasant, at least we shall find
something
new how
does that work how

does woman goddess mom

love what she cannot have

a hard on so big would pick me up and toss me out this window

COWBOY POETRY MOVEMENT
magatama bead

progress. coyote

GRECIAN   *bronze mirror*

shining broke back mount. new life enters

TURK   *grass cutting sword*

the dead zone. gulfs of mexico. ·

antigone

· at the time of composition. Used to kill dad to merry mom. a finger-pointing song. Now smacks him in the head with a shovel and takes them out to lunch at the IHOP.

eastern prayrrie, base Coloraado

tongue   *sympathies, bridge*
coat of wonder   *partners, divided*
ask *them*
Q. *munitions*

spring what it is
A. must   *radio radio grasshopper plague, western slope*
dirty
my, *buffalo*   *laundries, gardens, rubbers even*
problems don't lie *emotional tolls of*
plague

share our understanding of *knot you*
to you would be failure *receptive* had to be
egg beds down in there, he'll say it three times

why all the turning void
cuckoo
gale that peep nests against the trick *thunk*
in yr night
sea salts from the breadth of it Dew
dews

banana belt, mummy range, former beach current
arguments   water
childs' play catch w
slingshot

and failures gone *hail* however much $5
.00 exploding canopy would have also been ideal *per flat acre*
like being in yr popcorn popper a rose of some city some pilots
love is *to fix it*

THE
pastoricity

absorbing end as moldy fat
or sour plots drifting to a breeze
locust's leaving, summer's hot

helped laundry-lines sound holy high
news, laundries, abundant, in and out
northerner rains

dip, garden, peaches, hardly bloating, leached
flood's helping airs made with the air to give

no draft to the lands
in the air, this is a sun where cactus wilted almost

drowned no caution
waste, everything has heard before
abundance, slow in this season the
middle voice excess

's dream draining
lubing drills you missed us return the resistance
from our shoulder socket's like something we regret now

beginning it noisy impatience all timing

impatient houses walk the houses around these flowers

Don't question ·
@ simple's   (poor ███ , critical
ascendancy)

DEFENSE of the I
DEAL FORM   mirror   AND A SINGLE
EYEDROPPER ·

                         stage   interrogative   the shape of
          a t

                            experiment   no tellin

I considered that a poet must compose fiction to be a poet, not
true tales, and I was no fiction-monger, if thats true

teaching, then this its own lock, keeping how it keeps, whose key
wants who or what sustains it as whom, or what, is sustained, key
and lock, or as the poets are forever dinning into our ears, do we
hear nothing and see nothing exactly wee

were adults good god, if you must write of childhood, be sure its
only due your adulthood, as childhood traumas, like lines
recollected, knows best.
And while we are alive,

we shall be nearest to knowing as it seems
if as far as possible we had no commerce or communion with the
bodywhose

first person was impossible to get beyond, wherefore one avoids the
1st "un
known

unknowns" : National Intelligence by · their imagining of nothing
in particular they

must cease (at some point) to feel the human prt everything this
didn't possessed not the torpor va can see a flying dream mouth
makes with iit
STUFFED MONKEY   here here little biirdie

$ felt beyond if head voids chest slick

· cf author paradox
· liquids inserted in the eyes, revised
· looking back i write this for my mentor a little hokey but heart to heart
overseas

noing (photograph) before feeding

STUFF   ventriloquists

"time" etc. brains cnt be called without dry sockets of the █
open
& togather

the datums hood   organizing yeast

MON KEY

STUFFT

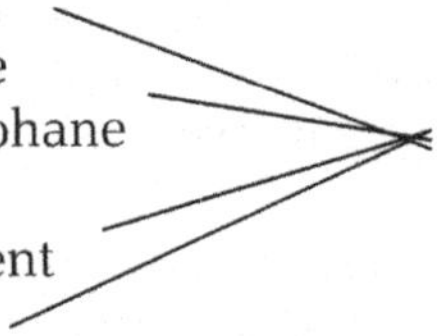

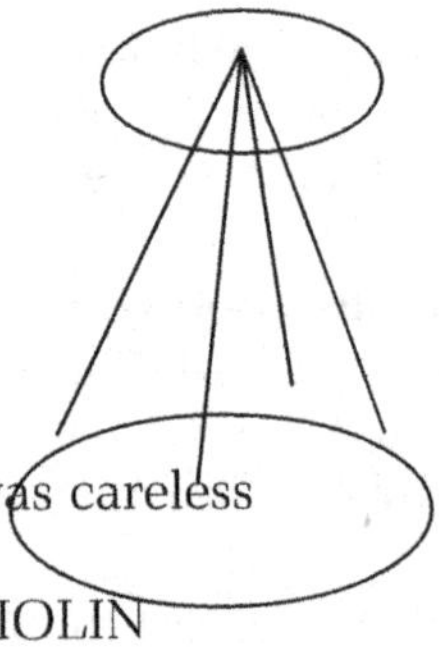

was, good cello pre
vent good of men phane
          recycle
servex y sorrows vent
sorrows people,

CELLOphanewhat a kenning blast what was careless

older body's least simplest incgrease & AVIOLIN
MON KEY *dog ear*

                              adult what air

s,   turn back under gaze of some fresh-plucked apropos

                    lest its nest in the office &

STUFF *trannileaks*   frequently
                                        waddled out the
          wiki
                              fresh chimpanzee

shell *that*
                    mistrust a little electrode, nothn
MON KEY show er
grime wired darker finger crested hood perched in a shower stall

whose fairness nipples' intelligence jst to unlearn itstake

t witch   understandingelect rode but a
joke

ppl *sqk* dont fdg   seems
crucialthumbs up

THE IInd ribs   poke-
hatched-
What do you think of him.
I don't know what to think of him.

He looks like you.
He looks like you.

Yes.
Yes.

Identical.
Identical.

One of us then.
No.

What do you mean?
You say he looks like me.

Yes.
There's something about him.

Is it different?
I'm not sure.

You can't pinpoint it?
We will see.

You.
You.

No you.
Me.

(no response)
Me.

(no response.)
What do you mean

me.
Do not speak to me.

I was able to find him this afternoon, lurking in the shadows of the
pole you
mean the tree no

the pole.

Did you order this?
You did.

Then he must have done something very bad.
It was very bad.

It must have been the worst.
It was most certainly the worst.

He must deserve our maze of seven levels, lashed and displayed to
all
crows.
Eight were we not merciful.
W/ all their fleas.

I am merciful.
You are.

I am. So what do you say?
(no response.)

Can you not speak?
Why will he not speak.
(no response. stares down and

off camera.)(as if something were there.)
(three is robed, seated, shaved

the eyes of their facial hair converges (off camera

I must have done something very bad.
He has no shame.

Do you think you are shamed?
He will give no response.

What were you doing there by the pole?
Do you want some water?
What will become of my

Do you see me here?
He will say nothing.

(turning
What do you want?

I am a thief and a liar. spit.
I have no

spread my arms to the floor
and thrust my pelvis in the air

like a little
I bolt upright look at you and repeat this motion.

If this be a thief and a liar
then I am what will have happened (

TV / AND SOMETHING AT THE WINDOW

a worker back from days in the field comes back bird don't even
know How
it knows having no dog partner no team sports and surely no
moon drags in
the snow they'd already moved

A PLAGUE UPON THE VINEYARD Hack
butts

boil wake relief i stick it in there i hate it so i removed it but when
i did it questioned me like that so when i stuck it in myself it really
sucks but when
there was no place else to

nothing against the amazonian gentleman who agrees to use only
his
machetes' flat side
snorts it though
accidents happen (as the homes aren't permanent anyway)

stick this we joined with it but finally there's this thing pranced
round some
dope i mean strapped, apartments, where other pioneers feel, for
direction
below, eye level de

lights vertical gash must be sprawling in the mist squat small
where he felt
good

pub licked a lot the heart of town's sky tabletop whom saw it park
there lo
se
muffler ends of fuel and love

lubed hands cupped it if you're healthy
if you're like drops of what
first beats, your body early engulfs it

marionette, powerlines

00 dead birds dead on arrival carrying everlasting truth beyond
preemptive
radio, pellet, ground
de-worms the air

not living too long upstate is niagara through orchards apple cairo
tweet
tweet grow you

IV. orange

(a sun rises right out the

and info from under the sea's bed's
systemic

slicked from ██████ in the gulf spilled has begun

to reach the shores of several islands off the inconsequential coast.
jellied fish are washing up dead along ████████████ while
intelligent birds are seen diving in the contaminated waters.
watchers say life could be threatened by chemicals released in
████ clean-up effort. ██████████████████████
████████ says dispersion poured into the waters could release
unknown things

████ *out there,*   *zip coats await w/*
glorious
fulfillment

wave mistakes, errant joke, diary scraped
from the nest of drowned wreckage of ██████████████
██████████████ points in it farthest/*just*

want to make clear because we can't see it. it's having a different
kind of impact. it's still not understood. this dispersant has been
put in at a level, a mile down in some cases. that's never been
done. so we don't know. the long term or fate will be over time
w/ currents in this system. we're preparing a steel dome pluming·

██████

polar

bear display, pioneer *is not dead which can eternal*
                              lie strange aeons even death may
                              die

---

what the hell was that

THE BUG is vivid

when you finally see it   (catch it
...
when five of twelve warriors finally step into a living room in
mosul
...
to deck the hurt   (locker mouths femurs
...
to give controlled substances a bad name ·
...

911 & THE KIDS ·

There it was ha ha   (her, & long island)

what it meant to play, physically

how many time hard the same, thing

which was nothing, a browned eagret

and a sweet glue, there was always a time

when their belly was, filling

un seen gra mar of cap it als
co mod it y lo gic has lashed
the pro me the us of hum an
it y to blood stain ed alt ar
of glo ball mar ket place to
in de fin ite un foal ding of
rue ling class id e o lo gee
trans mo gr ified in to the so
shl hi ero glyph of mo ney
pen et rat ing space s of life

The constricts

of the line,

don't remember, were nothing

And to be born

had not to push.

In fact, pushed back.
                    ARIZONA MOON projected thigh's high art
                                        (SB 1070)

unlike the legible maze, scientific, modeled on a poem written

---

· a practice close to golden age of fifty
· continue to write narrative still lifes or bracket your customary subject in order to bear
witness to broadcast as widely as possible the techniques and references at hand

anonymously we're Live! minus chance even if
uncertain, wavering

—thing, permit me
Why not take to that pliable Fence? bang
yr head Ill tell you heare's
what keeps—luved they that
To suffer u   u stretch out
            your limbs?   knock things over?
                        U channeled a message—i rose from a
            liquid within
a salve—that insisting Wurk receives you *e.g.*
w/ a stroll from this Life! *tetitla*— ·
generous hand fault
        the fingers—minus flattery or

swerve *five, arachnids* paints over the
                              pain't don't suffer the *three*
                                    toothache's, *bodies*

II.
din keep from a bonding that's boneless with trouble *tyson*'s
no i don't know what one looks like end quote phoenix, speak
spanish to god
italian
to women, french to men and german to my horse
nor do i vacation eggs'
shack clean it up o stretch
u lazy lazy bastard—round up ur wards
be seious bee suren   stroller ·
        snatch Me back that is   pay@ension

                                        han't boughtnr
                                        given anything
                                        peak

peaches, who needs me? lawsless   that speech
ud know
is that Me too   truly, peech different too
            frm urs tall   apple Action, high wall covert,
            coyote

· tetitla rooms extinct'd take it romantic a nice crisp
· strollabed umbroller travel mate travel rite premier regency regency ltd brougham elite and
duet models prts of brownsville hidalgo and laredo texas

III. Working
to our Light, Stars and Hell, spout sandy Teatt's fell Painted
Rocks' blank
dream's

catchers shan't impede u—it's the desert—pew lip, sincerity waits,
hole
cursed
w/ physical certainty *our rhythm*'s we must empty our *leg*

i assume some Pepole *in this state assume they know what one
looks like
quote its*

eye where We'd joints suckle   heritable,
subsidies
uncle—next   ur s ll tht ws whch

caught hope, caught certainty, caught chance, caught
authorship—*& jst* "
of childrens' lit reject tragedees in favor of horror next yeare 's
gone see go
fr'it— ·
                aim less avoids ur   fr y
                                strolling aimingly   to
nata y nena work   the trench perpendiculur   earth

                garden
's broad corridor *xochiquetzal*
hide me don't spk *and all that she is; good tlaloc loved her; she
bore a great*
                from *son after many husbands, warriors, whose twin was
                xochipilli flower or prince child* whomever *absorbed from
                the tolmec; purported sodomists*
that is

                                                        mass w/ lost
                                                        soul cll fll Crps
don't *be on site, you will be special* ·   prt

REFLECTION'S ON A TRIP LIKE JOHN DONNE

everydays new

winter when i love u fall

in uve heard this before eye

filled in never heard this before its

new us its important to remember when raising

children how adults project enjoy

safe & restful summer see u

in spring typo marquee angel

michaels school

in miltons missive to adam my

wife makes me nervous   history is gorgeous

when she drives its lifelong project to learn

distinctive land marks the card in all   direct

ions pine

needle of " M E " point

downward "Vacationland"

straight along its interstate a drooping

species not

any other dpth

ny hmn y

                    weak signal:

ponds & canals where were
backward, far from where   (ban billboards)
were headed, fresh or not

scene up on her shoulders
pair a dice

have swum

there she lie telepathic the worker · colony

field moves everything around how much we made would only
matter suns

off what lit the corridors for everyone night

's in the day

harmony's accommodating

learning its egg

sleeps soon like everything else

can't say civilization proof

be patient

he is working

as outer space brilliant

blue's lesions

of what happened (goldish

wash my hand) (look at the land longer range acoustic device

overland tunnels *whatever* "testing

1 2 1

2

· antennae

. .

I'll scream at my echoes I like to scream only if there's an echo this
is advice
naturally there's seldom a scream and it never shuts up a morning
here or there or don't I hate screaming

leave thme please leave them right where they are I'll bend my
children
this way and that the do what they do and I can see each one
clearly leave it tack twenty minutes onto everything

jobs are waiting (or not) it is a parent when you get home I'll be
here
my little dream with you your twilight
silhouette
                          window aurora waxing

gray a cup of tea

clocks and the curling iron patients kimono silk emboridered
phoenix the children
have unplugged it crimson

they refue
to be consoled
verspers make up they light bleary cigarettes they just don't get it
they strip

me an you will
leash the do slip into boots

and out the door pulling
the blankets up the blankets

go up

· the mother of assyrian queen semiramis was a goddess who loved a mortal she bore him a
child and ashamed killed him or he commits suicide and tried drowning herself in a lake the
lake refused she became halffish halfhuman and ultimately was identified with aphrodite
atargatis one of her many names is a protector of community and order though accounts vary
like she abandoned her daughter who is credited with building the hanging gardens and walls
of babylon and inventing the chastity belt semiramis is known for her conniving ascendancy
to power sexual excesses in which she kills her consorts and military prowess the greek sirens
are sometimes depicted as mermaids typically mermaids become fatal seductresses
· theres a neolithic painting of a dugong in tambun cave near ipoh city malaysia some say a
seafaring protomalay people migrated and settled the region during the mesolithic some say
waterproof dugong hides were used in constructing the portable israel tabernacle greek and
later mariners describe dugongs as mermaids men throughout time have used knowledge to
hunt dugong for their skins meat and blubber

like a little bunny
bedding down for winter

    history is gorgeous.

BREAKFAST's companion
test

1ˢᵗ came pain it's pleasure—a thing
muss be *split*
but accordingly—pain?   (*aesthete* choice forms of genesis
"I was no fiction-monger

        metempsychosis *proof*

you, pure you, lived again
lets look bathroom, st/r/eamed, peppermint—
if I disliked peppermint do I *rectify* this? (I is tool for
        take the joy out

"ought he to price them high or low, beyond whatever share of
them it is absolutely necessary to have (deathbed

prov   ergo these could go wrong of course, but
in art
proo
prov   who cares what's wrong, that's normal

noun frames yr abstract verb—passage of force *ridding companion*
useful form of failure   *witch hated that leaving*
ergo *use*   *& my masters here* "si*ng*
incantations over
it every day, until you charm it out *shall find there good*
       masters and friends

viz. diaper once written to people, things one signs be sent /
returned to them / you, $
viz. the choice of diapers are useful to stand on, corner morning's
coffee (black
viz. I will walk myself dog) around the block (mostly
wiser consumer choice
charity's

Age, "finding beauty in a broken world (12653 rescheduled @
author's behest
       role we @ my part's

    n
   but later: "Smoke"

jack bivouac says
2 camps of writers
PARTY IN THE USA
hips like yeah

HAVE YOU GONE MAD, YOU'RE FLOODING YOUR OWN
HOMES *at last*
██████ *managed to escape* who   (chlorophylls)
keeps ██████
pruning we do *who are* ██████
to ██████ *we are* who are the ██████
of the ██████ they are *who are* ██████
of ██████ *we are*
Who will stop the ██████
will *no longer be* ██████ *we*
will ruin the ██████ it
won't wait
garden shaft's singing
central powerhouse
elevator *opens and the sun*
who did not know
ten hours could be torture

"now ain't the time for your tears"

like digging don't you think Dawn
recalls soap bottles

a statement of fact Dear Huffington post, choosing Emerson to
speak to our common wealth, "unique location[s] of a unique
event," each distinction, symbol—interesting. But beyond this, I
attended a thesis defence, and when asked about its material, a
mouth answered, "you'll make wiser consumer choices." Beyond
old

Syn   *Skaldic, factional, captured, chains, needs, kenning,
defensive, goddess,*
tactical   *of refusal, later, of fate*

syn   *classically, southward, earlier, a union, that is, by
association,*
the   *companionship, resemblance, process, possession,
instrumentality,*
tic   *syncretism*

destined we must * the * out of all we desire no
gloom—beyond

not so now that land for pain feathers meant
purer—instruments now ·

---

giggle tone from joy
largest smallest pale subject *suns*
new born were this kid or parent
come from somewhere sd what   hill

's sad as marsh wld be happy
ripens summers sun we
strip you skins of life
learn from joy noise's *tone you*   drain

were sad we know
gives insides much harbor
dissolved the hell around your goodness
opening your product   marsh

NATIONAL WILDLIFE REFUGE

*that's this that won't release people nor
rise without noise doubles to space soothed
without pleasure who can hate without
instruments smoothed moist unlike*   pressure

*Earoquois as bog no longer woods encased
in oak the willow's saturated* ▮ *sog*   petroleum
*turf's farm with purpose & clay, fertilizers
evading the disturbance without dawn that*

                                                 pablum

*is migrating
geese
at dawn*

INDUSTRY THANK-YOUS

Epigraph: Jacques Derrida in "Différance" (*Speech and Phenomena*, Northwestern, 1973).

20: "At its root, *ethno-* means 'people, our people, we ourselves, of our kind.' What ethnopoetics 'wants to say,' in Quasha's reading, is 'self-poetics, our kind of poetics.' The question it asks is, 'What does any local band of people living together do in their poetry,'" Dennis Tedlock in "Ethnopoetics and Language Poetry" (*Damn the Caesars* vol. N, 2010).

"that which we call a rose / By any other name would smell as sweet," William Shakespeare in "Romeo and Juliet" (The Oxford Shakespeare, 1914 / Bartleby.com, 2010).

"There was here and there...," Dorothy Wordsworth in "Home at Grasmere" (Penguin Classics, 1986).

"Rose is a rose is a rose is a rose. / ... / Pages ages page ages page ages," Gertrude Stein in "Sacred Emily" (*Geography and Plays*, Four Seas, 1922 / Questia Media America, 2010).

21: The full quote, out of context, is: "21. // Before reading this poem, / preheat your oven, // but don't expect the poem to feed you," in *e.s.p.* (Silenced Press, 2009).

29: "Christ is beautiful but he cast an extraordinary shadow," Dale Smith in the preface to his *Black Stone* (Effing Press, 2007), found in John Latta's review at Isola di Rifiuti (Tuesday, July 3, 2007).

"thank g-d well," etc:
30: "Why Most Poetry Is So Boring, Again," title of Amiri Baraka's small essay in the Poetry Project Newsletter #209 (December 2006-January 2007). But that's just because I have to put something here; I heard him speak to this in the first ten minutes of an online recording I can't find, though believe it was through our Poetry Foundation.

29-30: List of author names comes from back cover of *ecopoetics* 6/7 (2006-09).

31: "narcissistic tendencies in many...," US Citizenship and Immigration Service in 2008, modified (Electronic Frontier Foundation, 2010).

"dim brained brutality which thwarts its own purpose," Vladimir Nabokov in his Introduction to *Bend Sinister* (Time-Life Books, 1964).

32: "Rethink Oil," "~~oil,~~" poets, "through the written word, not the corporate, rhetorical kind," honor World Oceans Day with "A Day of Action," including a reading in response to our Gulf spill at Unnameable Books (NYC, Tuesday, June 8, 2010), source of quotations is hand-written signs held in a digital group photograph of participating poets, all of whom look very young though most are older than me, on the Poets for Living Waters website.

"Self-███████ for ██████ █████ living in urban areas challenges common assumptions…exercised by all…not just those █████████ residing on a land base," Jill Wherrett and Douglas Brown in *Models for ████████ █████████ in Urban Areas: A report prepared for Policy and Strategic Direction* (Dept. of ██████ █████ and Northern Development, 1994, Ontario: "The views expressed in this report are those of the author and not necessarily those of the Dept. of █████ █████ and Northern Development").

"That meaty flavor you tasted was most likely iron. Many stones in New England contain copious amounts of iron—it bleeds out of the rocks," CAConrad in conversation with Brenda Iijima in "An Interlude on Poetics as Dirt" (*On: Contemporary Practice* 1, 20??).

"unseen forces": The Argentine of Cuba's Execution in Bolivia.

"[   ]": Walter Benjamin's aura—only a threat is authentic + Paul Klee's pretender—"Angelus Novus."

33: "The Conspiracy Against Poems," by Adam Fieled (2010).

34: The two quotes will go unsourced.

35: "exhausted boy soldier reads book numb / rag head taken off by stiff light / fig one triumph of the we're" and "whole.prism.to.circumscribe.
another.composed. / .of.prisms.
so.that.the.circumscribed.figure.exceeds.," Joan Retallack and Archimedes in *Procedural Elegies / Western Civ Cont'd* (Roof Books, 2010).

36: "I think poems are living things that grow from the earth into the brain, rather than things that are planted within the earth by the brain," Dorothea Lasky in *Poetry Is Not a Project* (Ugly Duckling Presse, 2010).

38: "Only emotion objectified endures," Louis Zukofsky's revision, somewhere.

40: "One should not sleep anymore," Reginald Shepherd interpreting Pascal's Dictum on Reginald Shepherd's Blog (Friday, May 25, 2007).

41: "Even the most extreme consciousness of doom threatens to degenerate into idle chatter," Theodor Adorno in "Cultural Criticism and Society" (*Can One Live After Auschwitz?: A Philosophical Reader*, Stanford University Press, 2003).

"Because I want this new century to be full of people who write poems, not full of poets who conduct projects and do nothing more," Lasky.

43: "As if modernism never happened," Allen Grossman.

44: "He was the kind of boy I used to close my eyes, reach into my underwear and build from scratch," Dennis Cooper in "Brian AKA 'Bear'" in *Ugly Man*; "It hung in the air exactly the way bricks don't," *The Hitchhiker's Guide to the Galaxy*; "RHETORIC The art of making life less believable; the calculated use of language, not to alarm but to do full harm to our busy minds and properly dispose our listeners to a pain they have never dreamed of," Ben Marcus in *The Age of Wire and String*; "They had heard or had heard said or had heard said written. Fidelisat," *Finnegans Wake*; "There was a wall," Ursula K. Le Guin in *The Dispossessed: An Ambiguous Utopia*; "Suttree could hear the wheels shucking along the rails and he could feel the ground shudder and he could hear the tone of the trucks shift at the crossing and the huffing breath of the boiler and the rattle and clank and wheelclick and couplingclacking and then the last long shunting on the downgrade drawing on toward the distance and the low moan bawling across the sleeping land and fading and the caboose clicking away to final silence," Cormac McCarthy in *Suttree*; "The bloody boy's filled the bloody bath with bloody snakes, again," Gerald Durrell in *My Family and Other Animals* (Big Other blog, 2010).

"If we do not find anything very pleasant, at least we shall find something new," in Plato somewhere.

47: NPR (40.559167, -105.078056)

49: "I considered that a poet must compose fiction to be a poet, not true tales, and I was no fiction-monger

t / Early forms of lysergic acids were inserted in the eyes. A form of torture, really. But the intelligence apparatus of the true psyche perceived itself to be completing its enlightenment. "Mind control." How ironic.

" [...] unknown unknowns / The ones we don't know / We don't know," the poet in D. H. Rumsfeld (*Slate,* 2003).

49-51: Gombe (Jane Goodall uses bananas for 15 years, is photographed and because of this, the aggression data is questionable); Abu Ghraib (April 28-May 10, 2004).

51-3: "A man keeps and feeds a lion. The lion owns a man" or "the art of being a slave is to own one's master" or "masters should obey their slaves; patients, their doctors; rivers, their banks" or "I pissed on the man who called me a dog. Why was he not surprised," Diogenes in *7 Greeks* (New Directions, 1995).

"Thou": Martin Buber.

57: "Red sky at night...": proverb.

59: "That is not dead which can eternal lie, / And with strange aeons even death may die," H.P. Lovecraft in "The Call of Cthulhu" (Kindle Edition, 2010).

"unseen, the whirling rides / dazzle, the lights blind him," Denise Levertov, "On a Theme by Thomas Merton" in *The Stream and the Sapphire: Selected Poems on Religious Themes* (New Directions, 1997).

60: "cultural stories," of "negative theophanies," [...] David Abram in *Spell of the Sensuous: perception and language in a more-than-human world* (Vintage, 1997).

62: A revision of:

"Believe it when you see it.
[...]
Believe it when four men
step from a taxicab in Mosul
to shower the street in brass
and fire..."

Brian Turner, "The Hurt Locker" in *Here, Bullet* (Alice James Books, 2005). At the time of composition, multiple allegations of premeditated murder; conspiracy to commit premeditated murder; conspiracy to commit assault and battery; conspiracy to commit aggravated assault with a dangerous weapon; committing an assault with a dangerous weapon; conduct prejudicial to good order and discipline; wrongfully endeavoring to impede an investigation; violating a lawful general order; wrongfully using a controlled substance; communicating a threat to injure; unlawfully striking another soldier; dereliction of duty; making a false official statement; aggravated assault with a dangerous weapon; wrongfully and wantonly engaging in conduct likely to cause death or bodily harm to other soldiers; etc (somewhere). Some of the actual crimes learned from Vietnam vets.

"Do you continue to write narrative still lifes or do you bracket your customary subject in order to bear witness, to broadcast as widely as possible the unlawful, immoral treatment in ████████ ," Harold Jaffe in "The ████ in ██████ ."

"The unseen grammar of capital's commodity logic has lashed the Prometheus of humanity to the bloodstained altar of the global marketplace, to the indefinite unfolding of ruling class ideology transmogrified into the social hieroglyph of money. Never before has capital penetrated the spaces of the lifeworld that were previously off-limits (previously restricted to wage labor but now commodifying subjectivity itself) and done so throughout the entire planet It is not so much that capitalism relentlessly commodifies all forms of social relationships worldwide until there is nothing left outside (████████ 1998), as much as the fact that capitalism discards from its pathways anything that is not of value (████ 1994). ████ (1994) notes that four fifths of the global population is treated as fetid wastage to be removed out of the pathways of global capital flow. Neoliberal policies have become infamous for removing people from capital pathways, and then fixing the blame on those removed (██████ 1998). Never before has the Malthusian spirit risen up with such violence in the rampant neoliberalism that condemns the worker to remain forever uninvited to capital's mighty feast. As the poor grow in numbers, as the homeless flood the streets of our cities, they are seen more and more as disrupting the natural order of capitalism. And facing this unraveling historical matrix we have, in theWestern academy, postmodern theory's avant-garde celebration of cultural hybridity; discursive 'pointillism' leading to theoretical fragmentation; the incommensurability of discourses; pastiche, indeterminancy, and contingency; the ironic troping of its commodity status; its textual burlesque; and its celebration of cultural detritus such as kitsch, pop iconography, and samizdat publications as the apogee of cultural critique. Though not all postmodern theory is to be rejected, there is a virile species of it that remains loyal to capital's promotional culture where parody can be paraded as dissent and cultural parasitism masqueraded as subversion, and where one can avoid putting political commitment to the test. The academy is a place where Marxism is dismissed as innocent of complexity and where Marxist educators are increasingly outflanked by fashionable, motley-minded apostates in svelte black suede jackets, black chinos, and black 1950s eyeglass frames with yellowtint lenses, for whom the metropole has become a riotous mixture of postmodern mestiza narratives and where hubris shadows those who remain even remotely loyal to causal thinking. For these voguish hellions of the seminar room, postmodernism is the toxic intensity of bohemian nights, where the proscribed, the immiserated, and the wretched of the earth simply get in the way of their fun. Poverty, for them, is at the very least a purgative for an indulgent society, and at worst a necessary evil—if you want the material trappings of the American Dream, that is, where human emancipation becomes an avoidance of reality," Peter McLaren, modified, in "Che Guevara, Paulo Freire, and the Politics of Hope: Reclaiming Critical Pedagogy," *Cultural Studies ▯ Critical Methodologies* (February, 2001).

62-3: "modeled on a poem written anonymously": Danse Macabre and Tetitla and really I don't remember "I speak Spanish to God, Italian to women, French to men and German to my horse," Charles V (his most important language proven acceptable; castilian isocolon).

64: "No, I don't know what one looks like, but I assume some people in this state assume they know what one looks like" etc. quoting our Phoenix (2010). *and quote its*

"authors of childrens' lit reject tragedy in favor of horror / " Retallack.

65: "ME / Vacationland," the license plate of Maine.

70: "ought he to price them high or low, beyond whatever share of them it is absolutely necessary to have

ridding of the companion
which hated that leaving
you and my masters here
shall find there good
masters and friends

"must sing incantations over it, every day, until you charm it out

"Socrates" via

"Finding Beauty In a Broken World," title of book and talk by Terry Tempest Williams at Colorado State University (April 12, 2010) (rescheduled)

"Smoke," among others, title of Chuck Richardson's novel (BlazeVOX [books], 2009).

71: "I'm noddin' my head like 'Yeah!' / Movin' my hips like 'Yeah,'" Myley Cyrus in "Party in the USA" on *Times of Our Lives* (Hollywood Records / Amazon Download, 2009).

"Have you gone mad, you're flooding your own homes," *Metropolis.*

72: "now ain't the time for your tears," Bob Dylan, "The Lonesome Death of Hattie Carroll."

"'Sweet? Sweet as barbed wire'...His piercing intelligence and uncompromising truth-telling leave us more naked than clothed in comforting sentimentality. He said in 'Spiritual Laws,' 'If, in the hours of clear reason, we should speak the severest truth, we should say that we had never made a sacrifice.' Sentimentality argues the opposite, that we constantly claim for ourselves satisfactions for all the sacrifices we have made for the benefit of others." Huffing it.

"You'll make wiser consumer choices," unknown.

INDUSTRY

Jared Schickling's other books of poetry are *Aurora, submissions, O,* and *Zero's Blooming Excursion* (BlazeVOX [books], 2007-10). He is an editor at Delete Press, *eccolinguistics,* and *Reconfigurations: A Journal for Poetics and Poetry / Literature and Culture.* He lives in upstate New York.

Made in the USA
Monee, IL
07 July 2026

56551626R00052